To Dona

AGAINST MY WILL

Cecelia George

TO SOW IS TO HARVEST

Scythe Publications, Inc.

A Division of Winston-Derek Publishers Group, Inc.

This
Body
I
Don't
Remember
as
Mine

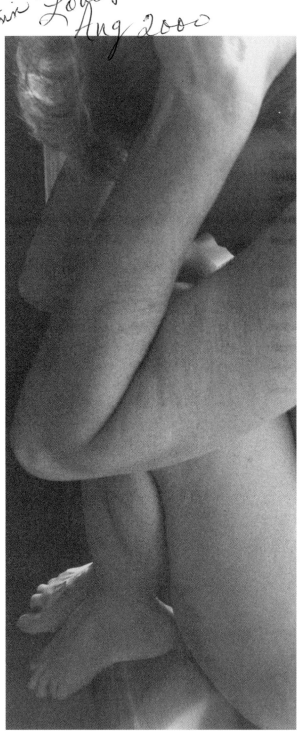

PUBLISHED BY SCYTHE PUBLICATIONS, INC.
A Division of Winston-Derek Publishers Group, Inc.
Nashville, Tennessee 37228

Library of Congress Catalog Card No: 98-061214
ISBN: 1-55523-871-8

Printed in the United States of America

Table of Contents

Offering

Opening – *Why I Write*

Outcry

Private Room Please

The Cold Before Dawn

Offering

I offer you these pages
with hope for your healing -
know you are not alone
suffering.

Some poems you may not like
or connect with
but if one word
welds together
the confusion and loss
of chronic illness -
I count each word
a blessing given to me
    to give to you.

Opening

so little I know
only a word
an opening to light
ever so gentle

through streams of weeping
sunrise beyond knowing
caps the morning rose
pure
silken
tender
standing tall in the breeze

Why I Write

A man asked me what is the purpose of writing poetry,
holding readings, hearing poets recite their work? I was
silent on the phone, wanting to express why I write.

Because... I want to show you the wild iris in the woods,
lips spread to the wind in shades of purple,
yellow splashed in just the right places,
seedlings sprouting among the black stumps in soot,
deer silhouetting in and out the ravaged forest,
rabbits hopping from bush to bush,
the sky a lake so blue umbrellas me.

I want to tell you I had French bread and milk-duds
for dinner, wanted to make love in the woods
when no one was looking. How insignificant I feel
standing next to structures stretching to the sky.
How the wind whips tangles in my hair, cat tails
wrap around trunks of trees, that incredible feeling –
letting go with the wind walking.

I write when I cannot clutch you in my arms
and nothing makes any sense, when bombs are falling,
mothers are dying, my son lost to his own addictions,
illness eats away the platform of my life,
and ice cream melts in the freezer.

Because... I want to tell you how it is for me walking
the streets of Paris and Florence, floundering
with my faith, gazing up to creation with all the passion
of purpose, beads of light flow through my pen, my brush,
camera, the words I cannot sing, cry or shout!

Choked up wet from weeping, I write
when no one understands my penance swallowed on a chain,
when angry days of clock watching dry milk
from supple breasts, apples turn green in red skin,
the phone rings and no one is there.
I hear Bach's Passacaglia playing on the organ,
sun streaming through stained glass.

I write when I am overjoyed and preludes play
Pomp and Circumstance to my dreams,
the enclave of voices singing in the night,
the written word... testament to my expression
scribbled in all the corners of time,
touching the places where no one can go
                    but the words from my heart.

Outcry

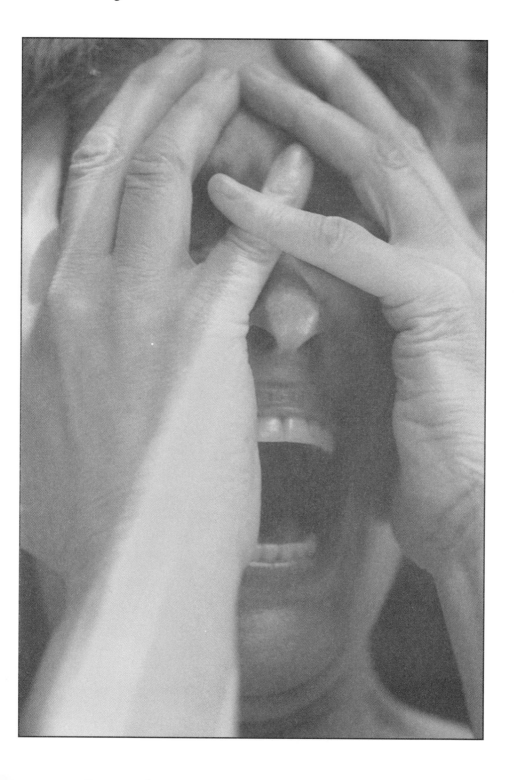

Chronic Illness

It comes as a thief in the night
as a rapist who lies on my body
holds down my will
chokes tight my breath
strips clean my pride.

Terror fills the night
sieges forth a gust of fear
ramshackles the space
that feeds longings to the wind.

A cast of heavy air
stagnant across the silent sky
rages in waking cells
bare
against my flesh.

A flame of remembrance
pierces the stirring
what lies ahead
days in bed stolen
with black gloved hands
slick around the clock
that stop jewels
from glowing in the dark.

The river dries skin to the sun
rain trickles finger troughs of time
swirls a small trench through mud
too shallow to swim
too far to run
too dirty to see
the robber's reflection
caught in a scream.

From Memory

She looks in the mirror
touches her pale skin
with one finger
traces her face
an elegant line down
her long slender neck.

Frail shoulders unshawled
naked to the bone
bend around thin arms
hanging to hands
swollen with sickness.

Fingers burn
a burden to carry rings
where life circled nights
across lean legs,
feet too weak cast still.

She sits by the window
wakes the early dawn
in glazed silver light
she brushes her thinning hair
              falling golden.

Deception

If I broke my leg,
was in a cast
and had a crutch,
everyone would say
"What happened to you
are you all right
do you need help?"

If I were badly burned,
wrapped in bandages,
everyone would say,
"What happened to you
are you all right do
you need help?"

If I had an accident,
was in a wheelchair,
had a patch over my eye
or splint on my arm,
people would notice

My illness is invisible.
I often look fine
so people don't know
I'm sick, lonely,
need help.
Nobody says,
"What happened to you?"

Relentless Intruder

below the surface
pain pierces the place
where rats ravage the traps
in dark attics
and I hold my breath
waiting for rain

hail pounds the window
rails louder than thunder
cuts beneath the savage siren
thrusts the bones
pushes sanity to remember

pale autumn mornings
crisp leaves
lean winter days
spring showers
soft summer evenings

light sparks
where pain grows
into the night
delirious stabs penetrate
deep
disturbing the quest
for rest

Dialogue With My Right Hand

Why is it YOU that is getting so weak?
You know how right handed I am,
how I love to write, garden, photograph,
move the bow across my violin, play the piano.
It is difficult to play left handed melodies
on the piano, or make notes on the violin
with just my left hand –
no one will hear the music without my bow.
It is so painful to hold my beloved pen,
I suppose I should learn to write
with my left hand – BUT I DON'T WANT TO!

My dear Cecelia – I know how much you miss me,
I'm not even pretty anymore, you can't wear rings,
you keep me covered with a glove
because I get so cold. Do you think I wanted
to become red, stiff, with swollen, ugly fingers,
not having the freedom I need?
Please don't be mad at me – it's not my fault.
If you let me rest more, not force strength
that isn't there, I could give you more use.

I know I'm getting weaker, my grip losing focus,
please stop pushing and squeezing me –
I want to heal so we can create together again.

I'm trying, I'm trying,
but I use you instinctively
without thinking until you scream at me!
I had such hopes these new drugs would work,
but it looks bleak.
I cannot stay on chemotherapy
and I know that it will be even harder on you.
We'll try other things.
I'm fighting hard to get you back.
The doctors say I fight too hard,
do not accept my body's limitations,
I'm making things worse.
I'm going to a healing service tonight,
we'll pray especially for you,
even though my liver needs prayer,
my legs and arms.
But you RIGHT HAND
I'll hold close to my heart,
cover you with silken soft blankets –
       and we'll hear the music together.

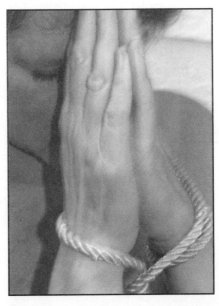

And I Thought the Disease Was Bad

My favorite pills are the orange ones
shaped like fat M & M's - but without chocolate.
Only mild side effects - abdominal discomfort,
vomiting,   diarrhea,   dizziness.

The white dog-bone shaped tablets
slide down easy, remind me of my Dalmatian.
Very dangerous – can destroy the retina of eyes,
cause blindness, low blood pressure,
anemia,   hearing loss,   curled fingernails.

Pink and white, the tiniest pills are most deadly.
Bloat the body like a sunken ship, cause ulcers,
hypertension,   cataracts,   glaucoma,   osteoporosis,
facial hair,   blood clots,   diabetes,   insomnia,
mood swings,   hallucinations,   insanity, to name a few.

Long white hard pills nurture nausea, constipation,
skin rash,   headache,   blurred vision,   kidney damage.

Pretty little blue pills can cause cancer,
hair loss,   dehydration,   depression,   fatigue,   weakness,
fever,   liver toxicity,   gout,   paralysis,   seizures.

Soft gold gel caps and clear white powder
damage the liver and the mind.

Big, bright, round, yellow disks increase blood pressure,
edema,   headaches,   drowsiness,   bruising and bleeding.

This potpourri of pills I take is really rather risky.
I grab a handful – toss in over tongue
water down with metamucil.

Who knows – I could live to be 100
if I can still stand,   swallow or see.

Mush Anyone?

My life has come down
to a bowl of mush.
My gut snaps at my sanity,
hot cereal dulls the pain,
soothes the demons
dancing on my navel.

On good days
I eat soft potatoes, carrots,
bites of chicken breast.

Disease and toxic drugs
devour my dreams
of pizza, pies,
and french fries.
My special pan
to cook mush is wearing out –
just like me.

Chronicles of Chronic Illness

Monday I get chemo injections
Tuesday a tumor biopsy,   lab tests
Wednesday endocrinologist
Thursday neurologist
Friday Stanford Hospital
a new experimental drug
Saturday the psychiatrist
Sunday I pray

Between appointments
I squeeze a small life

Monday I start all over again
Tuesday dental surgery
Wednesday cardiologist
Thursday gastroenterologist
Friday dermatologist
Saturday rheumatologist
Sunday I pray
Monday I start all over again

Usually Positive and Upbeat, But Today...

I'm tired of pain
of hurting everywhere
eight years now
I rarely complain

I'm so very tired
being sick
smiling, pretending
it's not so bad

I'm tired of resting
pacing myself
remembering to remember
not to move like a bomb

I'm tired of bills
insurance claims
doctors, appointments, long waits
X-rays, urine specimens, lab tests
I want my blood back!

I'm tired of feeling bloated
a blimp,
no salt,   sodium
or sassy sauces because of pills

I'm so tired of missing life
living indoors,   no sun
no late night movies
a run on the beach,   hiking
or dancing parties with friends

I'm tired of being tired
swallowing handfuls of pills
for stomach aches
headaches,   feet aches
my heart aches
for dreams unspent

Blazing the Blue

My disabled parking placard
bright blue
blazes I'm handicapped.
That word scary
embarrassing at first.

Well, everyone has a handicap.
Some people, totally self-absorbed,
have no compassion
their disadvantage is worse than mine.

My legs may not be strong and sturdy
sometimes I think a little slow,
but if anyone needs some loving
or sympathy - I'm here for you.
My eyes and ears are not disabled
my heart will hear you weep
sing or laugh —
and we'll dance on blue water.

New Parts Please

Another week, new ailment
eyelashes to toes
I tread on a wounded knee

win the prize for pictures
vital signs in black and white
A different doctor,   conductor

for my orchestra of organs
Some pitched high,   low
others cool, clammy, calcified

Diversity of disgusting parts
that refuse to function
as formed

I'd like to trash this model
start next week
with a bright new body

RPMs revved up in red
I'll roller blade
with a brand new knee!

Success Story

Her smile ear to ear
fills the magazine picture
doting children and husband
surround this "superwoman"
Mayor of Marville, chairlady
of every board,
she gardens in her spare time
carpools the kids, jogs
has a personal trainer, beautiful home
energy endless, a success story –
she holds all the stars.

I did it all
until disease devoured my life
transposing choice.
Today I boast of accomplishments
sweeping the floor, washing my hair.
I hold on to self-definition
inner calm, because I can no longer
rearrange myself to what I was
smiling – in a frameless photo.
Boldly I catch stars –
spread boundaries for a new life.

Private Room Please

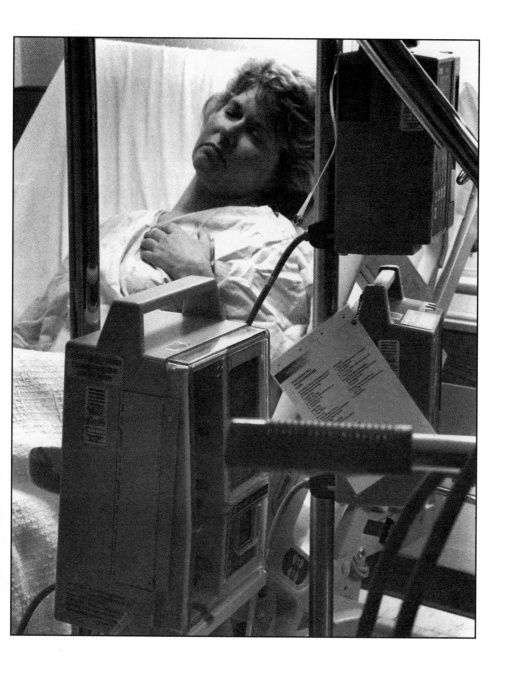

Wanted: A Private Room

I'm in the hospital
it's midnight or one A.M.
I can't see the clock.
My room is a tiny cell
in the overflow ward.
We are bunched in like bananas
spotted, overripe, some rotten
some green with no color
I try to sleep.

To my right is an old man
no teeth, mouth dropped to chest
moaning, coughing, very sick.
The young woman on my left
sleeps soundly
through her own coughing
lights glare on her face.

Nurses talk loudly, telephone rings
copy machine bangs, doors slam
deaf patients yell for attention.
I feel the pain of prisoners
stacked in windowless cells with dark walls
at least these walls are white.

The overflow ward is really a supply room
with medical equipment, gaping machines
stacks of light bulbs, cleaning supplies –
no bathroom, telephone, T.V.
windows or roses.
My view is bed pans and blankets.
I try to sleep.

My I.V. and oxygen wires
tangle and strangle my arms
bantering for a warm place to rest.
I sleep three hours.
At 4:30 A.M. loud booms the voice
of the respiratory facilitator
waking my neighbor for her asthma treatment.

The old man on my right throws up
goes into a seizure, almost dies.
He is moved to the I.C. unit.
It is quieter now but more bleak.
The darkened, cold room
fills with heavy breathing and coughing.

I am not sure when morning creeps
between sterile white walls.

You Have Great Physical Powers and an Iron Constitution

Peking Noodle Company

I wait to be admitted to the hospital
for yet another procedure to keep
my ailing body "pinned" together.
Needing a laugh - I find this Chinese fortune
taped to a page in my writing journal.

Well – since I have such great physical powers
what the hell am I doing here...again?

Now – if the Peking Noodle Company means
great physical powers like wiggling my toes,
holding a cup, brushing my hair,   talking,
clutching my pen in pain to write –
then boy – I'll be an Olympic finalist!

As for the iron constitution, the Noodle Company
gets an A+. A constitution so strong
I can move mountains, raise a barn in an hour,
lift a tank, part the seas.
My iron will has kept me alive for eight years
and I thank the Peking Noodle Company
for a great laugh amidst needles, biopsies,
I.V.s – and grim-faced doctors.

Poke Gently Please

I bet you've had it too –
days and days of diagnostic tests
hours waiting in paper blue gowns
(Barbie would barf)
skid-free slippers, plastic bracelets
dye-marked veins, gaping machines
scans to scare a cat
coffin tight tomb
hammers drill in your ears
needles, bands, barium
every organ showcased on screen.

Nothing to eat or drink since midnight
I scream for ice cream
my stomach growls, I dream of donuts
                    and a rose satin robe.

Annie

An old black woman with a beard lies in her bed
watches me walk slowly down the hospital hall.
I wave as I return to my room next door to hers
she smiles faintly and waves back.
I ask the nurse if she is male or female
not seeing clearly from a distance,
the nurse assures me Annie is a woman.

The next day I wave again as I walk by.
She smiles bigger, her wide, electric eyes light up.
I say "Hi," she smiles back broadly
but not so big I might see she has no teeth.
She keeps her door wide open,   lights on
mostly sleeps, but catches my eye anytime I walk by.

Later I go over to her bed and chat
ask about the machine she is hooked up to,
inquire how she is feeling.
After a brief visit, feeling my own exhaustion
I say, "Goodbye, I'll stop in after dinner."
She says "Goodbye DARLIN'."

Annie and I seem to be alone in this huge L.A. hospital
reaching out to each other like lanterns in the night.
I sit with her as much as I can
hold her hand, listen carefully, try to understand
her toothless words, her praise to the Lord.
She loves to talk - I love to listen.

Each day she looks stronger
though more dialysis, one kidney already gone.
Annie and I bond between machines
doctors, I.V.s, pills.
She walked only once, a few steps with her walker,
I was there to cheer her on –
to help with her hair, the nurse shaved her beard
we got her looking so good.

I leave the hospital as Annie is wheeled into surgery,
kiss her beautiful cheek
let go of her hand as tears come.
This old black lady from Arkansas touched me with her love
her sweet, sweet innocence.
I can hear her say "Goodbye DARLIN' - I love you too."

Chemotherapy

It's been a "cracker year"
crackers morning, noon, night
    and snacktime
brown rice, pink rice, wheat rye
saltless, tasteless cardboard
crunches across my face
tumbles down the place
to soothe the sour taste
the stirred up stomach
gurgles and hisses
rebels in the night

This drug of eminent reputation
kills the creatures of cranky protest
shuts the cells and cuts the smells
nausea the wave of the present

It's easy having a "cracker year"
no creative cooking
no hassle, no mess
just boxes and boxes of crumbs
sliding down my mouth

Soon I'll eat a chocolate cake
and make a cracker crust pie!

A Smooth Ride Please

Two days ago I turned fifty
today I had my first ride
in an ambulance
I'm in a hospital
and need to be transported
to another building down the street
for special tests

The ambulance was an hour late
it was in an accident with a taxi
I was spared the drama
The two cute blonde drivers
in charge of their slick
orange and white vehicle
moan about their baby being hit

We laugh a lot
as I'm transported six blocks
stacks of paper work
for such a short ride
they take vital signs
I lie in a belted bed
a bumpy ride in the back

I like the girls' big black boots
strong bodies
I suggest they get a Dalmatian
to enhance their image
we laugh
fill out more paper work
they check vital signs

Two hours later
I am back in my hospital room
with memories of a new experience
tucked into a brand new decade

Wrong Ward

The maternity ward
noisy as a zoo,
children bang doors
clamor to see new babies
mothers lecture mothers
fathers tired and worn
children cry,
 "mommie mommie"
a weary couple bicker.

In room 2220, I'm alone
wearing a recycled
pink flowered maternity gown
faded, with pressed ruffles
that conform to full round
nursing breasts for baby.

My flat narrow breasts unbound
lie quietly empty.
I feel the place of pelvic womb
where seeds of reproduction
have been emptied out,
laid to rest.

Gracious gown of motherhood
binding my body in the wrong ward
I bequeath to you in serenity
the sorority of frazzled faces
I'll sip tea with roses
hear the cry of falling leaves
linger in the mist of morning –
celebrate the tranquil night

Into Light

Under squares of fluorescent light
she quivers with nauseous chills
the I.V. pierces her delicate vein
drips streams of liquid life
into a body screaming profanities of pain

Hands move round and round
the clock times her pulse
machines drum a low hum
voices mutter numbers in the night

Warm blankets nurture her commitment
to get up from the table
leave behind knives and needles
run to the cool damp forest
climb the old oak tree
caress a smooth long limb

A limb that knows the endurance
of pelting storms
antiqued in tones of golden leather
laced with new green veined leaves
shining in the wind

draped with moss and pearls
crimson berries and nuts

Quietly she calls
the creatures of her imagination
birds on her shoulders scatter seeds
fly into beams of light
under circles of sunshine
her body quivers with wholeness and joy

The Cold Before Dawn

The Cold Before Dawn

the song lulls on leaves
brown from early frost
frozen
feelings thaw slowly
through fingers of time
touching the nerve of fear

voices drum sentiment
in dusty corners of church
empty rooms in dark memory
where candles flicker
the flat stone of silence
coats the cloak of night

clashes in cracks
savage bleakness hurls words
back to bitter ground
cries in winged bellies
born deep in black trenches
bares the vision in shadows

out of this despair
courage
undresses remnants of light
the cold before dawn
collects pain
holds the dimness
bitter sting before the sweet
soaks ripe in blush color

wind sails soft hands
the robin flies beyond clouds
sun shines through mourning
dusts the weeping rose

I Don't Have the Choice Anymore

to hike, bike, run... somedays I can't even walk.
Disease has raked up my immune system
into compost piles collected in every
corner of my fragile body.

I don't have the choice anymore of what to eat,
drink,   wear across my swollen belly –
my feet scream at my shoes. Sometimes I lose
my hair, hearing, myself... in the battle with drugs.

I don't have the choice anymore which pills
to swallow to stay alive. So many losses
I wander through the maze to find the exit to myself.

I don't have the choice to play Brandenburg
Concertos, or dance the tango, but...
I can hear, see, smell, smile, remember
the feel of violin strings under my crippled
fingers – transpose to gently cup my camera
and capture tulips and iris standing
with arms open reflecting the grandeur of simplicity –
orange peel, cinnamon buns, windchimes,
tick of the clock - song of your voice.

Behind Walls

I live behind the walls of this house
they steep a slope of forgiveness
my heart at the door, I wait
for shadows to fade into blue

noontime in the garden with you
my hat blooms in the sun laughing
this illness buried in rows
dug by hands patient from waiting

behind the walls of this house
the world spins on bright windows
in corners where wind dashes dust
clocks chime on the hour day after day
counting not one sparrow forgotten

I remember feet dancing in green
lilacs on walls climbing high
the dream flashes faster and faster
time twirls on the tip of a rose

in winter nights bleak with cold
behind the walls of this house
no farther to look than the room
waiting and waiting dark hours roll
as streets melt with the living
graves bloom in light on peach scented hills
behind the walls of this house
I'll dust away crumbs
and borrow for bargains of time
cast still in this body
       I don't remember as mine

My Birthday
I

My eyes catch the first light of morning,
of time capsulized in caplets of fear.
Puffy face tries to find once slender cheeks,
every system attacked with disease
that destroys my dignity, my independence.

Hopes for healing blur away.
Another year older – so ill –
but still… the tall slender girl
running barefoot in the sun,
climbing trees, baking birthday cakes.

I call my spirit to carry me
through the maze of misery,
thin threads hold me together.

I bask in blessings through tears
of sorrow and loss,
linger with autumn leaves,
sit by the fireplace with friends, family –
cards and flowers bring joy.

II

Do I want to live for another birthday
even if I can't walk – keep waiting
for doctors to document a new treatment?

I want to throw away all pills,
NEVER see another doctor.

I hold on to every beam
of bounty within my sacred self –
plant one last red tulip as bruises bleed
into the palms of my hands.

Vigil

If I but wait a little longer
it will be morning
closer to the living
soft light through fog
dew on daisies
smell of coffee
a reason to wipe clear the night.

If I but wait a little longer
alone in the dark
no hand to hold
no body next to mine
or voice to calm the terror
in gentle reprieve
my eyes blank the dots
of a thousand nights kept
on dark shelves.

If I but wait a little longer
for bones to bend
heads to bow in prayer
the saints will march the road
untethered
sweeping glass from broken bridges
spanning the river of tears.

I drink from one cup
wait for morning
by the dim light.

Across the Bridge

dry, shallow breath
parts the parched lips
taut against the pillow
pain peels along veins
deep throbs drum the silent night
flame in rage through black tunnels

across the bridge of bed
on lacquered shelves of white
quiet joy - flowers,   books,   photos,   cards
respite from sharp stabs
crushes the sanity of wholeness
pushing patience through walls of waiting
I tatter a scheme of fortitude

last light of night hangs sharp
candles flicker, drown
luminating the ledge of reasons
that die hard in empty shells
clock stops within
I see the distant view of time
healing on the wake, so far to walk

my flat bed of illness surrounds the crest
I wrap my wishes in satin pillows
pain penetrates all parts of believing
tomorrow will dawn with dew on roses
ringlets of ferns,   feathers in the sky
sunlit streams

the flow of beauty ceases
buds wither,   blooms wilt
      plants wait for water

Depression
I

a stillness throbs in my head
despair hangs sleepless
my mind tries to find reasons
wanders through the maze of night
napping on minutes
searching for a warm place
I fold feelings under my pillow
push back bellows of time
swallow more pills
catch words lost on my pen
the friend I've cast away
song of survival sings again
if only for a moment
I collect another hopeless night
a week,   a year
waiting for revival
waiting for my feet to dance again

II

nothing makes any sense
books have no words
pages blank turn black
carrousels stop,   the horses fall
the music warps,   winds and winds
tune of truth blares in place
clowns stop smiling
babies don't cry
lemons become sweet,   meadows dry
the grasses grey,   an empty field
tulips dwindle,   drab color in the sky
birds don't fly
there is no rain

no laughter,   no voices in the air
no father,   mother
no people on the train

I sit in an empty ferris wheel spinning
sputter the word stop -
no one hears me

III

Dawn breaks the silent seal
survival through the night
the peck of birds on the roof
counts out time
taps a tempo of sadness
slow,   rhythmic,   rote reminder

I stare into space
spoon food across dry lips
lean on a ledge of insanity
dredge self to dress
a numb mannequin with cloth
wedged around tangled hair

I wash walls of isolation
wipe sweat from sitting frozen
a castrated call
the phone against empty voices
in my head
sounds march around my mouth
forgotten air grips my chest
taut against the clasp of hands

Strains of stitches hold the day
this dismal depression
dulls sun from shining apples
waxes faces a slick red
my smile turned down
body bent in distant pose
hidden behind sunglasses
all the discipline it takes
to walk outside in the light
step in front of step
I stumble
as I straighten tall

Waiting To Be With You

I lie in the still cool night
waiting to be with you
wanting the darkness to roll
into leaves of light.
I collect hours of waiting
under heavy eyelids
slanting up to silhouettes of shadows
dancing on my forehead.

I want to ride the last limb of light
to where you are
cradle solitude of singing songs
to white walls that pacify the watch
of ticking clocks – oh, the age of time!

Weary, the world rests its feet
folding flowers of the meadow at midnight.
Lullabies of sassafras and columbine
the net where nesting egrets
tuck their beaks in curling remnants
of straw twigs and ribbon fern.

A place I'll go to rest and hide you
on my back far away, where night walks
the moon in purple dress and circles
home in dew of morning mist.

Anger

Don't even look at me
and please, no pleasant platitudes.
I'm not going to keep my chin up,
just going to look at my feet,
kick, scream, pound my pain
into streams of steel.

No surrender, no smiles today,
hope lies low in my chest.
I carry my grief in a cradle of stone,
long years of illness glare black.

No chimes today, or music, no mustering
my strength or courage.
I yell for yesterday, tomorrows I'll miss.
I've mastered a plan for survival...
                              but not today.

A Rope and a Miracle

The steep mountain looms unfathomed ahead
I've climbed it many times,
my enthusiasm undaunted then
I pulled myself straight up,

tapered the toxic drugs for my illness
each step a slow rescind
to reach the pinnacle of purity,

my body fighting the cliffs
of precarious relapse.

The view at the top breathtaking –
exhilaration of arrival rewarding.

I was getting well until rocks hit hard
knocked me down,   I lay in a heap
forced back on drugs.
I climbed the mountain again months later.

Each time I fall cells crack,   splinter
my long slow climb I work so hard to make.

I'm at the foot of the path again
going up - I'm afraid,   unspirited
need focus and hope.

Discipline and desire to heal give me a push,
one foot in front of the other.

This time I need a rope,   a band of angels
                    and a miracle.

Early Hours of Morning

ebony hours of early morning
when night calls dawn

time beads on branches
melts
damp color on arms of lace

skirts of night's cloak
swirl clouds in sheaths of fern
blankets of light
glint mauve across the sky

at once
day's fragile hand beckons
the moment to fold in comfort
safe respite of rest

soft stirrings on wings
mist the birds in flight
stillness fawns the cold

blooms unfurl
coral   amber
ascend
in sun's radiant seed

Time For A Break

Time For a Break

So sober,   pedantic,   my words
No joy,   laughter flow
Through this pen

What happened to animal crackers
I used to eat
Canoeing down rivers
Ukulele and song
Catching butterfly wings

So serious thoughts
Have formed
The grass will grow back again
I know

Pass the popcorn
It's time for a break
Race the ice cream truck
Meet me at the pond

Put some salt in the sugar bowl
Short sheet the bed
Loosen the lid on Grandma's
Joke box
Send balloons if I should die

Pack your picnic basket
And save the last dance for me

Always On Monday

I need a little smut
in my life
a soap opera day
X-rated night
Harlequin novel weekend
a smooch in the back seat
of your car

bright orange toenails
a tattoo by the flue of my rue
sexy lace
dangerous liaison with Danielle Steele
bedazzled in bed in a brawny blur

clamor for the glamour
chocolate in diamond studded dreams
juicy blonde on a silver cloud
bursting the air
in whimsical obsessions

a Cosmo cover girl
bosom beauty at the beach
secrets at the Ritz
pearls around my neck

zonked on a runner's low
I need champagne and roses
with moon beam's exotic glow
decadent indecency
caviar and crafty horoscopes
luscious pant on puffed lips
kiss me baby,   make my bliss
give me crazed erotic interludes
for a mundane mediocre Monday

Habits

My habits run deep
like the San Andreas fault
I floss my teeth
even after a major earthquake

With no power you'd think I'd sit quietly
with the glow of flickering candlelight
to ease my jangled nerves

but to the kitchen I go
in the dark
to flounder with dishes
sweep crumbs I cannot see

straighten stacks of clean laundry
that could be dirty
tidy up the night
in rituals of dark reverberation

Yes, my habits run deep
into earthen reminders of habitual nonsense

Will I ever leave the lint
dust balls,   cobwebs
scheduled agenda
splatters on mirrors, dirty stove trays
crooked bedspreads and lampshades
and enjoy an earthquake afterglow
soak in bubble bath
sip brandy and let the earth slip away

New Flavors

Time passes so quickly
I hope I have more living.
I haven't bought my Miracle bra yet
or tried cake mixes for microwaves.

Even if I don't get new shoelaces
that glow in the dark or
self-stick stamps
I want to see the sunset everyday,
cuddle a new born baby,
bask in colors of begonias,
feed monkeys at the zoo,
ponder wonders of creation:
tall trees
rain drops
blazing wind
an orchid bloom.

Modern and mechanized
every system around me now
I don't care about remote control
automated trash retrievers –
I just want to try
every flavor of ice cream !

Apricot Nights

I seek the serenity of simple things
satin binding on blankets
sheen of apricot nights
sunset spray in the sky
memory of my mind's eye
the apple bends within my reach
branches cluster dreams

in the wind I remember lean days
soft reflections and quiet interludes
I climb high enough to catch the rain
high enough to see the children play
I throw the string of my kite upward
                    in a loop
swing with stars through the dim light

I seek the serenity of simple things
the purr of the clock
candles in May
the moon mist
your hand in the dark

Mechanical Madness

It was one of those days
sitting with the phone
time on hold
        waiting
my head numb from voices
canned music in my ear
(Beethoven would be so lucky)
numbers,   claims,   account referrals
prerecorded mechanical voices
in robot staccato style
telling me what's for dinner

numbers 0 to 10
punch 4 if you need your teeth cleaned
5 if the oven's on fire
or wait until the next available operator
6 to bandage the dog's paw or cut his nail
7 if Bambi shows up in your yard
dust the droppings and press 8
9 will set your oven timer
10 for a nervous breakdown

and if you do wait
for the next available operator
maybe she'll share a martini with you
        and break the phone

Rat's Milk For Her Wrinkles

She died with a plastic bag on her hair
      sticky oil dripping out
thick mayonnaise on her long thin face
      an avocado down her neck

Oatmeal mishmush on her arms
red mud mask on her breasts
she was only trying to look her best
my God, at 50, what do you expect

They found her wrapped in mustard
mint jelly in her socks
carrot curls around her ears
cool ketchup on her rears

Elvis crooned a few old tunes
the cat lay at her thighs
licking lobs of creamy curdled milk
she used for cellulite

Her eyes were blue, so very blue
witch hazel spread on lids
her lashes satin long black hairs
dipped twice in chocolate beer

Heaven bound she bumped her head
kissed all the mirrors goodbye
tripped on her socks, oh what a fall
(covered with watermelon)
they found her in the hall

To Buy a Butt

They were hanging on a rack
at Fredrick's of Hollywood
  beige padding
to enhance one's derriere.
I am interested in trying one on
as I have lost weight
and lost my buff behind.
I have also noticed these buns
in the J.C. Penney's catalog
under "Special Needs."
Lovely Lift Support Briefs
to wear smoothly under slacks or skirts
with extra curves for rounder rears
made from soft polyurethane
sizes SMLXL – $12.00 to $18.00,
machine wash, tumble dry.
For now I'll settle for bony buttocks
or transfer fat from tummy
                              to tush.

Information Please

I stop and ask a hooker
where Thrifty drugstore is,
she says two blocks up Sunset Strip –
well,   it was at least eight.
(how would she know anyway)

I walk from my hotel in Hollywood
look for bottled water.
I'm here for an appointment
with a famous doctor —
am hopeful,
happy to be out walking
away from my bed.

It's getting dark.   I clutch my purse,
pass drunks and druggies,
glitzers and glamours,
every array of characters and stores:
The Body shop, Tattoo Jungle,
Exotic Follies, Sushi on Sunset,
The Comedy Store.

I laugh, walk a little faster,
pass the same hooker in her bright
tight orange and black attire,
tell her I found Thrifty's.
She laughs showing lots of big teeth,
her high heels clicking.

Lights so bright power the night –
I don't need a ticket to the Comedy Store.

I Love To Garden
I

I pinch back faded foliage, sometimes
rearrange pots packed with colors
crescendoing into sunny prisms.
I tell the plants how happy I am
to see them, tuck in stray limbs
water, sweep and sing.

Dressed in stoles and shawls
some flowers wear hats
others plump with crimson lips
some tall, thin, wispy in the wind
tendrils of green arms to cloak
lacy limbs of spindly spinsters
leaning unsteadily alone.

Eager each morning to see new blooms
I wait for my body to sprout new seeds.
My weakened immune system embraces
vibrant breath from each bright species
inspirits healing to grow –
I rejoice in the life I do have
even if I garden only twenty minutes.

II

My yellow snapdagons
snapped at me this morning.
What are you doing up so early?
You promised the doctors
to rest more – lie in bed late
not bend your fragile back
to fuss over us.

We are more hardy than you
need only gentle care –
please kiss yourself
sip some tea
and trust we will call you
when we need you.

For Keeps

This thick book of white spaces
    quietly blank
waits for curved markings
the memory of comedy on the road
spilled splendor of all the living
squeezed between the lines
mishaps in blue ink sketch
cries in the night
while flowers sleep
seeds spread and meadows grow
in playgrounds of green
red flies the robin breast
into night's kept land
my silent heart will grow old with you
    dear book
just don't fill up too fast

Alone At Death's Door

Bête Noire

the sickening sound slides
through the window
grey fog full of morning
saunters still across the room
the raven caw reverberates
resonates a quietus crow
on the rungs of my chest

orange walls awash in timbre tones
oppressive chords drone low
drive the piercing blackness
raven's eye turns a sideward slant
across my swollen lids
drills a call in regimens of roar

gripping fear pushes up the cavity of ribs
I lie in fixed pose by the open window
thrust blankets around my body
my ears rage in memory of the night
a sack of ashes in offering
the limb against my neck
twisted trunk of legs in pain curled up
across remnant of breath squeezing light
through cracks of silence

I grasp for the wing of its flight
silken shadow above this affliction
that claws at my sanity, pecks at bones
disturbs the night in unison voice
clinching to seep walls white
in terror I shake off the slack of death
sable raven in the distant dawn
                    wakes my dim cry

And...

the seasons turn no more.
Soon I will shed my leaves
be raked into piles for burning.
A heavy rain streams down
I float away,   find a birch tree
waiting – for my leaves.
I shimmer golden in the sun.

I know it will be all right.
I follow the white light –
hear the dove sing.

There will always be a sunrise
to follow the mountains east.
The deer call my name,
maidenhair fern and piggyback clover
bank the flowing stream,
I swim with roots bound upward
the sky covers my skin.

Blazing sunset paints pink magenta
across the hills
trees await ripen fruit,
orange blossoms garland my hair,
jasmine skirts my hips,

lilac plumes of violet light
                    lead me home.

The Light Beyond

Quietly the morning crisps the sadness
Frigid trees bare from winter's cold
Branches furrow the stark horizon
Calling light from peaks on snowy hills

Melting sounds of death,   iced
from holding on too long
Drift in feathered frost
Freeing life as dawn breaks day

Who Will Wake Me?

At first the signs are subtle
then sobs of sorrow pour down my face
bed blankets brace my body,   cover my head.
I lecture myself – get busy,   focus outward
exercise,   discipline,   get a grip.

Immobile, ill for eight years
a robot without reason
I stare in a mirror of reflection.

Where am I?   Too much face,   not enough hair
where's the sparkle in my eyes
long smooth fingers,   agile feet?
My smile perfected,   I hide behind laughter
jokes,   a mirage of memories.

My daughter's getting married soon
I'll wear a long dress and veil
hers white,   mine black,   we'll toast tomorrow.

Tonight I lie on my favorite toile pillow
papers in order,   though I need to clean closets
pay some bills. I find $31.89 in my wallet.
There are no fresh flowers in the house.

I fold the flow of breath beneath my pillow
count time on my fingers
until there is no more light.

No Longer Called

When I finally lift my weary wings
will there be any eternity left?
Across the sea
I leave my weathered shoes
to fawn the deer
no longer called
my shadow of skin covers the sky.

Circles of grass meld the dry earth
plum orchards prepare to bloom.
So much time has set the bones
yet I see a speck of bridge
beyond the hill.

I cannot walk anymore.
Will it help if I run;
if I stop to sleep
or watch topaz gardens
gather silent stars?

I lay my purple guard down
draw clear water to feed
the heather and thirsty violets –
dust the last repose.

Last Remaining Word

There is nothing left but words
and I cannot speak anymore
only sob and heave, shudder in silence.
Even the brown teddy bear sitting
on the T.V. stares at me in silence
his bell rung out, his eyes dolent.

There is nothing left but choked breathing.
My God I'm alone, shall I take all the pills,
fan out the fortitude everyone sees,
the smile that hides my grief?
Which way is the gate to hell?

I'm withdrawing my lottery ticket,
you can drive my new car –
cruise control with a cup holder
charcoal grey, the color of ash remains,
paint it red before I push it over the cliff.

There is nothing left, not even my tonsils.
I swallow my saliva in a tube of barium,
hold my breath,   breathe
relax,   now breathe,   swallow again.
Did you document the tears, count syllables?
Did the last remaining word
vex the X-rays in black trays?

I rehearse my lines,
mark the meter of waiting death.
This is no life, there is nothing left
but the clear cold night of black sky
sprinkled with stars
that dare to shine through my window.

Phone Call

The news came on Tuesday
six P.M.
Papa called
Mama is dying.

Numb,   I protect my fear
like the roof covering me
from cold rain
running down my spine
spilling into the cavity
of my heart.

If I were brave
I would shed my clothes
lie naked in the rain
until the news soaks in.

I look around my house
see her handiwork
the crazy jokes in the game box
hear her music on the piano
the bird's song in flight.

For in news of death –
we learn to live.

Last Breath

Gasps for air pierce sharp
the silent night
Moaning of the dying
chips far beyond the bone
Shadows fold in closing corners
waiting for that last breath
to spill out and shout

I'm finished –
Giving birth to death

I'll Bloom Violet

I pluck dead blooms
from my flowers daily,
ask if they
will keep blooming
when I am gone.
My body barely moves,
no smile,   no splendor of color
across my face
like the violets.

I replant when flowers fade.
Can I replant myself?
Will someone please pluck
debris from lifeless limbs
fold my frayed stems
sit a while – and sing.

My courage uprooted
clings
to the ledge for light.
When the sun comes out
I'll rearrange myself
unfurl
from valiant seed –
I'll bloom violet.

In Memory of Mother

You in a distant place
yet so close
your hand on my shoulder
memories enough to carry the breeze
to mountaintops glazed in sun
golden
with all the flowers you can hold
your arms surround the seasons
keep me now

To Begin Again

To Begin Again

I wish my feelings
could be free
Free like the surf
giving no excuse
for its raging waves
Pounding the shore
then gracefully releasing
its tumultuous energy
into long rows
of cleansed white foam
Moving to kiss
the sand
Finding its peace
to begin again

Once Again

The sand spreads before me
Silently
Like the new year
Unblemished
Yet touched by a million feet
Footprints reflect moon's light
Waves lull the shores edge
Moving into night mode
Into days,   years
Sand weaves a web of awakening
I carry my empty jar
High into another year

Priceless

I know my own value,
can I afford the rent?
Am I willing to hold tight
to my parking space here on earth,
let no one crowd me out,
or talk me into painting
my precious shell a different color?

I was born with big toes,
electric eyes,
a heart held over for others.
How much would I be worth at an auction?
Sterling silver,   14K gold –
Sold!   to the highest bidder.
Wait a minute – I can't be for sale,
I belong to myself and I'm priceless.

I walk down my hall of mirrors.
Can I ignore my flaws,
see ornate designs curved on my body,
intricate carvings embellished
with diamonds and jewels
sparkling in the glass reflection?

I stop, stare deeply into my eyes –
a woman worthy,   whole,
I wrap my arms around myself,
trust the torso that carried me this far,
promise to make myself top priority
and make sure my name is printed
LARGE on my parking space –
RESERVED – only for ME.

Coming Home

Everything in life takes practice
learning to die
living with moments
walking on dark roads
calling my own name

Giving birth to all the ordinary
in pain
humbled on knees
I learn to stand

Tall
in the rain,   alone
wrapping remembrances
thick around empty hands

In the distance
the sea whispers my name
over and over
fog plays gypsy to the wind
moon calls home
to the night

In darkness and light
clouds cover the rose
birds soar
higher
than I ever imagined

The song above the longest day
my breath repeats
the sound
no longer a stranger
at my own door

Affirmation

The silence
of my flaws
etched naked
under light
on mirrored walls.
Time erases
fear that runs
in wild places
chanting the brass
ring of doubt.
In solitude
with chisel
bit by bit
sculpted smooth
my face shines
radiant,   round
released
my hands open –
uncurling
the iron hold
of yesterday.

Returning

to the keys of my piano
my fingers follow the notes
notched in octaves and chords.
My stiff hands soften and curve
after many years - the music mute.

I try to sing along as I play
my breath encumbered
collapsing and expanding,
the words play their own song.

I remember when my heart was strong,
hands sturdy scaling the fingerboard,
lungs as bellows
forming rich reverberations –
renditions – "Memories,"   "Moonlight Sonata."
Mozart playing tag with ingenious scoring.
I chase him across the black and white
board of communion.

Tonight I hum melodies of remembrance,
my fingers,   magical as dust,   dance
and twirl, step the keyboard in tango.

The piano needs tuning –
I feed from the silver fork
the long strings quiver with joy,
anticipation polishes the porous wood.

I have found my voice again
even if my fingers are numb…
                    they know the way.

Dear Margaret

Let's not talk
about the hurts so much
the past
the whys
how come
how could he

Let's talk about
new days
today
what is
I am
right now

Let's talk about
tomorrow
dreams,   goals
I want to
I long to
I will

Let's talk about
peace
letting go
forgiveness
caring
understanding
Let's not talk
at all
just be
what we are today

Enough for Today

This word "love"
has become so complicated
so difficult to say
I choke the word up my chest
between the breastbone of my silence

I want to love simply,   purely
with trusting eyes
as I loved my first teacher
drawing colored pictures
singing songs off key
swinging with the birds
rolling in the grass,   giggling
roller skating home

to the gentle curve of mother's smile
warm as the creases she ironed
in my ruffled sleeves
cotton dresses,   homemade
pockets filled with secrets from the sky
glazed blue
love shared unadorned,   unaware
of all the whys

I want to love knowing
only the sweetness of today
holding hands,   hugging
living love without longing
                              for more

Blooming

I've come full cycle
with the trees
winter to summer
I shed leaves in autumn
bloom brilliantly in spring

I bathe in rain and
warm winter's fire
bask in sunlight
my leaves shimmer green
in the wind

I shade a place for sorrow
safe within my arms
where lovers laugh
and children play
secrets fill the air

I nest a bed for weary ones
call light from snowy peaks
my journey arches upward
bound deep,   I circle home

Tranquil Night
I

softly
the quiet night sweeps a wave
of serenity
across my tight chest

eagles,   owls
and night creatures
rest
as I on chosen branch

hide the dark
behind cold glass
piece the fragment of days
long counting

the rise and fall
of all that's been
as night collects
her calm

II

night wears her silken gown
folds fragrant blossoms
to her bosom
carries the sky in pink
and maple rose
circles the crest of hills
in peaks of pearls

remembers
across meadows in purple dress
blades of grass with dew
bend in day's breeze

night sleep-walks
wakes creatures of day
who miss night's serenade
sips lemonade of lullabies
rides falling stars
sings softly on satin scarves
                    of sleep

A Lifetime

When I left the trees were bare
    a month later
all are green and lush
buds bursting everywhere
jasmine, lilac, orange fill the air
How quickly I forget
sharp pruning cuts the way
for tender new regrowth
How come it takes me
so long to shed my leaves
    a lifetime
        to bloom a rose

When I Write

I am transcended to a place
where knowledge grows free as wildflowers,
opens wilted arms,   heals my heart
paints bouquets of flowers in dark corners.

It doesn't matter where I am
because I am already there.
My pen tells me what I need to know,
each word unique as a new specimen of orchid.

When I write – flowers never die.
Birds glide glistening across the sky
fly closer together, form a loving family.

Rain is softer – the earth opens her hands
and drinks from holy water.

There is completion to each day
a summary of my soul,   release
of knowing everything will be all right
even in the midst of illness and fear.

My words console me,   give me courage
to keep traveling even if I take only one step.

My imagination soars!
Words create a legend of laughter
a place to come and lighten up
angels fly, beckon my child
to come out and play...
I am safe within their keep.

Words replenish empty fountains,
fill wells of remembrance,   tune
strings of forgotten lutes
call me home when I can't walk –
carry me in gothic boughs of green
                    to my own cradle.

"Arranging a bowl of flowers in the morning
can give a sense of quiet in a crowded day,
like writing a poem or saying a prayer."
                                    – Anne Lindberg

When I Pray

it is like arranging exquisite flowers
in a tarnished silver bowl –
suddenly light shines
and illuminates the bowl.

I hear silent places – see petals
fall around angels' feet,
colors of flowers brighten
their faces open and sing.

Understanding confusion is not important
life is simple – breathe in – breathe out.
I see beauty in each branch
each vivid leaf, green hills in harmony.

I accept all my colors –
poppies, lupines, rich, red, Indian paint brush,
electric blues, gold flock the fields –
I am a masterpiece canvas.

When I pray a seed touches the ground
and I grow along with it.

Haven

I have found my place in the forest
far from city lights.
Squirrels, scrub jays, wrens
decorate trees outside my windows.
The cabin – a refuge from the realm of life
I live simply in the fall of my days:
linger by the fireplace,
climb rocks and roads,
breathe the peace of scented pines.
I wash my feet in rippling streams
whirling around pools that smooth
jagged rocks into silken stones –
centuries old, their story
is all I need to carry me home
when I have to leave the mountains.

Someday I will live here forever.
Someday I will be a tall blue spruce.

Freely as the Foxes Run

I want to walk slowly
through my garden of life
not missing one petal that falls,
a feather from one fragile
                        wing of breath.

I want to walk my grounds
                        as a peacock
fanning out my colors –
not exist as an empty stump
the foxes sun upon.

Let no one scare me into running away
                or hurrying my road
I will strut,   stare,   saturate
the air with granules of grace
given to me with each heartbeat.

For Now

I ponder life's meaning
stripped down
from too many words
beyond knowing
my eyes turn to the sky
stars write the story
one lash of light
one kernel
one blade of grass
a rain drop glistening

I touch lips with one finger
words blow to the wind
the dandelion dusts the air
words quiver in the night
tumble – stroking
the sunrise
falling to wet grass
soft   resting
in refuge from words
I close the book

Appreciation For

Jean Bennett, first mentor who took my writing out of the closet,
Laura Bayless, luminary, upholder… beloved friend.
Hannah Liebmann, editor – with spiritual vision beyond words,
Judith Harper – compassionate inspiration.

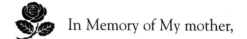 In Memory of My mother,

About the Author

Cecelia George, a lifelong professional violinist, teacher, former color and design consultant, unable to work because of chronic illness — Lupus and Scleroderma — now focuses on writing and photography. Her poems are published in literary journals and newspapers. She has won several awards. Her second book, *Paths of a Journey*, is nearing completion.

About the Photographer

Judith Harper is a photographer, printmaker, poet, dancer, traveler, hiker,movie watcher and daydreamer. "The object of my photography is to include the viewer in the picture. I believe my portraits allow one to be present on many levels and not just be a voyeur but experience the feelings, time and place in which the picture was taken."

To write to either of these individuals, please send your letters to

Cecelia George or Judith Harper
c/o Winston-Derek Publishers Group, Inc.
P.O. Box 90883
Nashville, TN 37209